HOW TO SCRIMSHAW AND CARVE IVORY

by Blackie and Michael Collins

Published by The Benchmark Company
P.O. Box 12121, Rock Hill, S.C. 29730

Most people who have heard of scrimshaw think of it as pictures scratched into the surfaces of pieces of ivory. True scrimshaw is actually represented by a wide assortment of art and craft forms which were performed with a similarly wide assortment of materials. Scrimshaw could take the form of various kitchen utensils which were carved from whalebone, the teeth of the sperm whale, or even wood. It could also be a simple scene scratched into the surface of a whale's tooth. The most significant identifying characteristic of the art is that it was performed by seafaring men who would use whatever materials were available to them. Actually, the word scrimshaw came from a slang expression which referred to the product of idleness or loafing. The sailors did indeed do their scrimshaw when there was nothing else of importance to do. It became most popular in the early 1800's with the advent of a serious whaling industry and died away shortly after the Civil War when the industry underwent certain changes in methods of operation. Recent years have seen a growing interest among collectors for articles of scrimshaw, and this interest has been devoted almost entirely to the illustrated tooth of the sperm whale.

Many artists are now producing a contemporary style of scrimshaw which is in some cases quite similar to the original work of the whaling seamen. Some few have refined and sophisticated this art form considerably, and offer their work not as a copy of the old but as a new style of their own. It is this new style of scrimshaw to which we direct our interest in this book. The sailors of old have taught us that the tooth of the sperm whale can be an excellent medium for the artist. This tooth of the sperm whale is a form of ivory and, therefore, other types of ivory are also acceptable to obtain similar results. The most readily available ivory is that of the tusks of elephants and this has become the most popular material for the new scrimshaw artists.

A single painting may be made up of thousands of brush strokes. So it is with scrimshaw. A single work of scrimshaw may be made up of thousands of cuts into the surface of the ivory, and in many cases, these thousands of cuts are followed by a very sophisticated brush technique in which the carved surface of the ivory is transformed into a scene of beautiful color. In this book, we will show you how some of the foremost practitioners of the art achieve their results. We will illustrate the methods, tools, and materials, used for creating pictures in ivory.

Unfortunately, ivory must be obtained from the most noble of beasts, the great sperm whales and the mighty elephants. Many restrictions have been placed on the import and sale of ivory and these restrictions are necessary if there is to be any future for these animals. We fully support any reasonable and effective efforts to offset man's frequent indifference to the delicate balance of nature.

BASIC TECHNIQUES

THE TOOLS

The tools of the ancient scrimshaw artists were adapted from items which were already in use aboard a sailing vessel. The heavy needles which were used for repairing sails were used for scratching lines into the surface of the whales' teeth. The tools in current use are usually made up especially to suit the tastes and methods of the artists.

There are two basic methods of scrimshaw. In one method (which most closely resembles the old style) the design is scratched into the surface of the ivory. In the other method, the design is cut into the surface of the ivory. There is a considerable difference in the results obtained by the two methods. The scratching method is accomplished with a tool which is shaped like a needle. It is usually round in cross section and the point is formed by simple tapering. In use, the point is forced into the surface of the ivory and moved about to make the desired scratches. The final image is brought about by transfering some coloring agent (ink) into the scratches to make them stand out from the unworked portion of the ivory. Herein lies the problem with scratches versus cuts. In order for the image to be sharp and smooth it is necessary for the lines in the surface of the ivory to be sharp and smooth. When the ivory is scratched, a mark is formed which is the result of a combination of depression (like a dent) and gouging (like a tear). The area into which the coloring agent must go is, therefore, of uneven consistancy in its ability to receive and absorb the ink.

Ivory is a very dense material, however, it does have a certain amount of porosity which makes it suitable for the absorption of ink. When the ivory is polished, the surface becomes more compacted and the porosity of the surface is eliminated. Ink will not be absorbed by the shiny, non-porous surface. The scrimshaw artists must expose porous material so that the ink will take and the image will be visible, but it must only absorb the ink exactly where the image is to appear.

Scratches in the surface of the ivory are rough and uneven and when the ink is rubbed into scratches it produces a rough and uneven line. At arm's length it is a little more difficult to see the roughness of scratches compared to cuts. A closer look by the trained eye will discover the difference readily and the true quality of the work is never determined at arm's length. The better artists like for their work to be examined under a magnifying glass.

By cutting our marks into the ivory we can control the width and depth of the cut precisely. We can be assured of better direction and an overall better and truer image.

PREPARATION OF THE IVORY

To prepare the ivory for scrimshaw we must polish the surface to a smooth and hard finish. In the old days the sailors accomplished this preparation by filing away the roughness and then sanding the surface with sharkskin. After the surface was sanded to an acceptable smoothness it was hand-rubbed with ashes to the final finish. The ashes were obtained from the fires which heated the tanks in which the whale blubber was rendered into oil. These ashes had a slightly abrasive effect and also acted as a type of filler which further reduced the porosity of the ivory.

The contemporary artist has available a wide ranging assortment of sand paper, files, and polishing equipment with which he can produce a much better finish in a fraction of the time it took in the old days.

The surface of a piece of ivory should be filed to a smooth finish and then progressively sanded to the finest grit which is available to the artist. Starting with 150 grit paper and working through 220, 400, and then 600 grit, will give an excellent finish for final polishing. This is best accomplished on a cotton buffing wheel with fine jewelers' rouge. It is very important that the surface of the ivory be actually smooth and not just have a highly polished appearance.

Scrimshaw artists will often perform work on pistol grips, jewelry, or other pieces of ivory which come to them already polished. It is always best to carefully examine the surface before any work is started. The seemingly fine finished surface might actually be full of small scratches which are not readily apparent. If these small scratches are not removed they might cause the artist to have to start over and sand away some of his hard work.

Anyone who has a belt sander will find that it is not necessary to use a file to establish a smooth working surface. We use belt sanders for most of our shaping work. When using any type of motor driven equipment, it is easy to damage the ivory by overheating. Cracks and checks in the surface can be caused by overheating and it is impossible to remove them. A good rule of thumb is to never let the ivory get too hot to be comfortably held in the bare hands. Do not cool the ivory in water so that the work can go faster. Ivory will absorb water and later it will dry out and contract. If it is used as an inlay it can shrink and become ill-fitting. A coarse grit belt on a belt sander will work much faster and cooler than a fine grit. It is best to do most of the finishing work by hand with sand paper. It takes longer but it is worth it for the resulting quality.

MAKING A TOOL

A good scrimshaw tool is simple and easy to make. The only materials required are a short length of tool steel rod and a piece of wood or other suitable handle material. The only tools needed are a file, a drill for the hole in the handle material, a propane or butane torch for heat treating, and a sharpening stone to finish up the edges.

The tool steel rod can be shaped with a hand file. File away the steel indicated in the illustration.

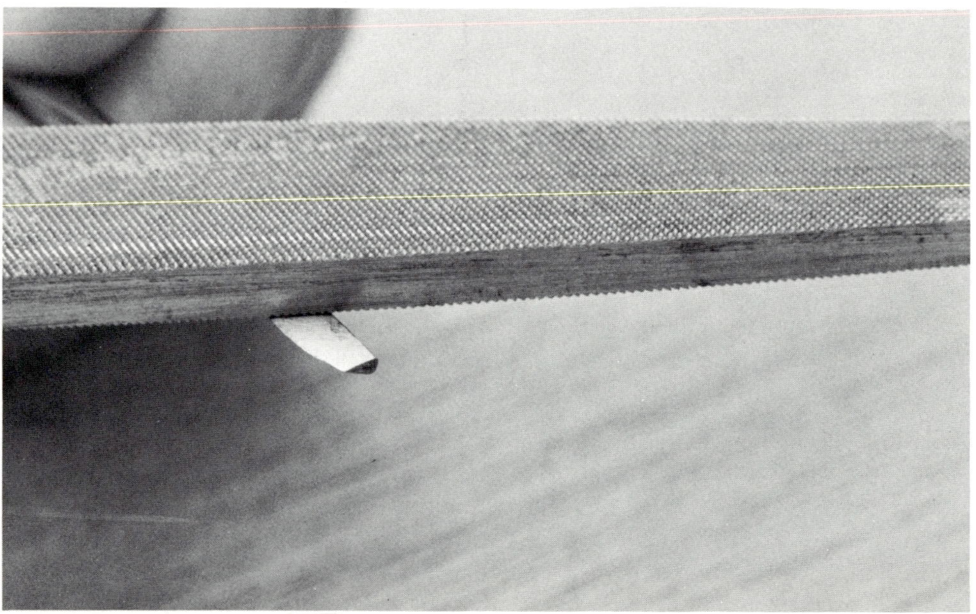

After the bevels are shaped and a short cutting edge is form-ed, the end of the rod should be filed off at about a 30 degree angle (sloping back from the tip). The end of the rough finished rod should form a triangular shape.

The rough finished tool is now hardened by heating the tip to a bright cherry red with the propane torch and quenching it in oil. If the proper temperature was reached, the end of the tool should come out of the quenching oil with a slate gray scale which can be flaked off easily. The hardened tool is too brittle for use and must be tempered. This is accomplished by using the same propane torch to heat the tip until it turns a straw color. Be careful not to overheat as this will return the steel to its original annealed condition. Do not quench the steel after it has reached the proper temperature for tempering. Allow it to return to room temperature normally.

The handle material should be drilled with a hole which will accept the steel rod and the rod can be epoxied into place. Shaping of the handle is usually a matter of individual preference, but a round handle about ½" thick and about 4" long is comfortable and effective. The tool should extend about ½" out of the handle.

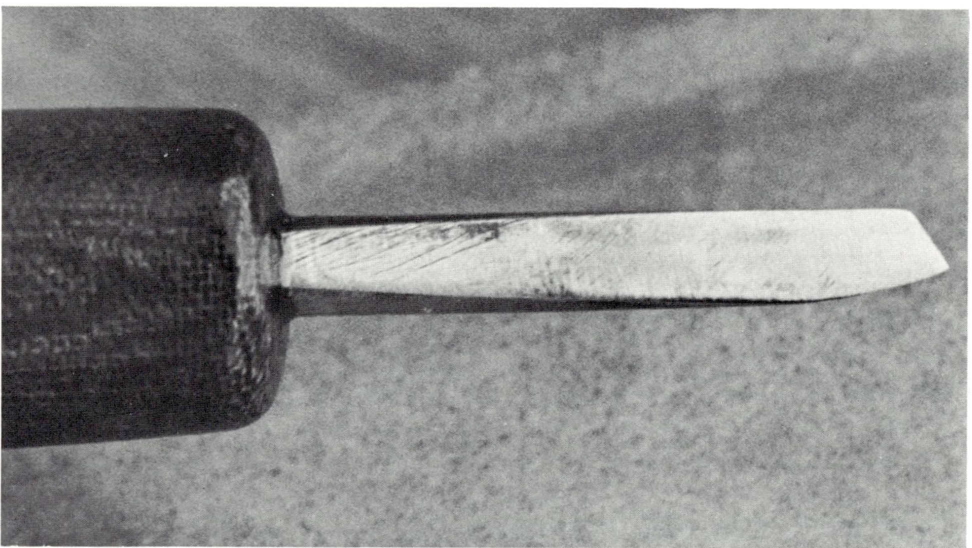

The tool can now be finished on a sharpening stone. The sides should be honed down flat and smooth and the end should be honed to a smooth finish also. The last ¼" of the tool should now be a sharpened edge which ends in a point where the three flat bevels come together.

Proper maintenance of the scrimshaw tool is a must. Sharpening should be frequent as the tough ivory will dull even the hardest steel. Constant checking of the tool will provide a much cleaner and better quality cut. A good way to check the tool is by placing the tip against the thumbnail and making a sideways movement with very light downward pressure. A sharp tool will dig into the nail and a dull tool will slide across the surface with no resistance.

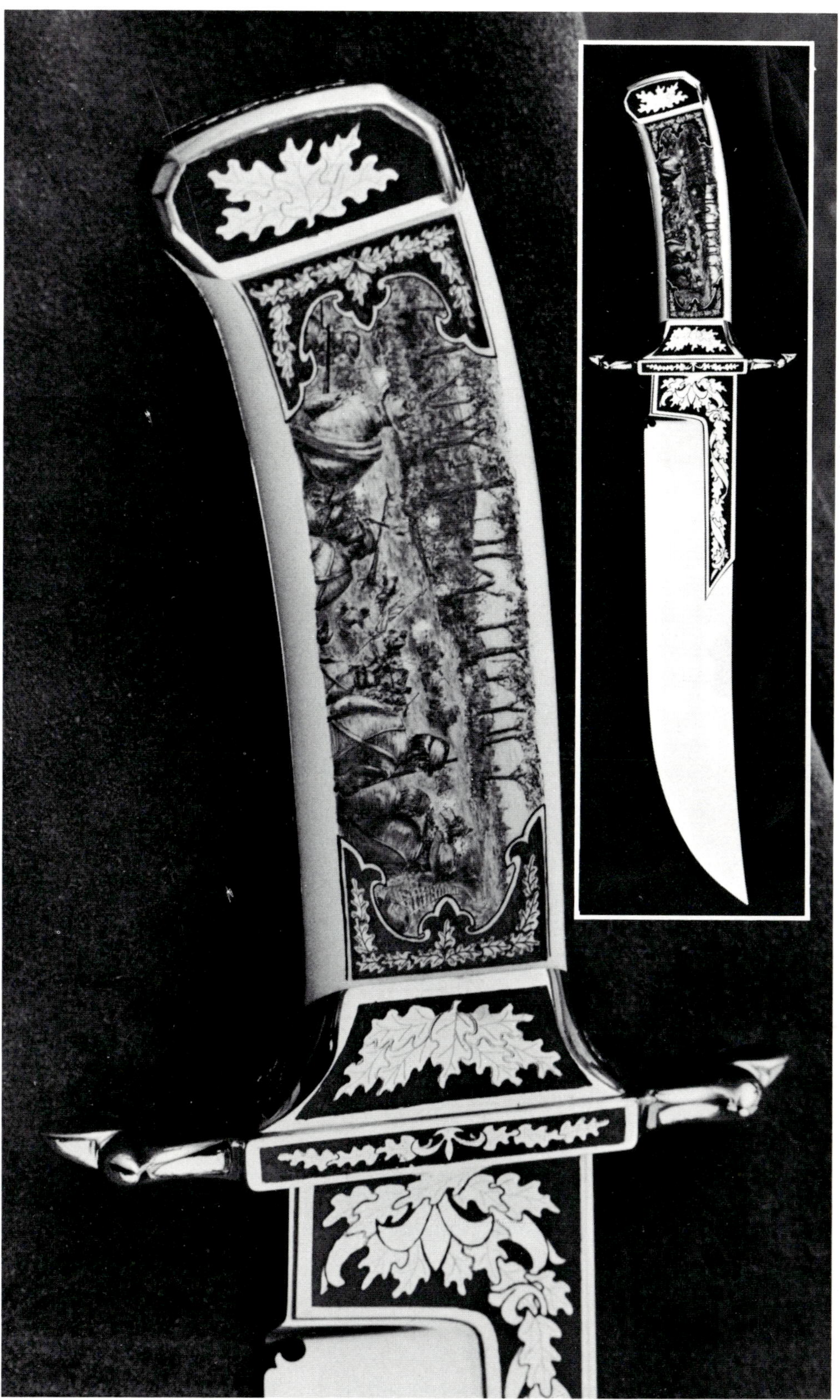

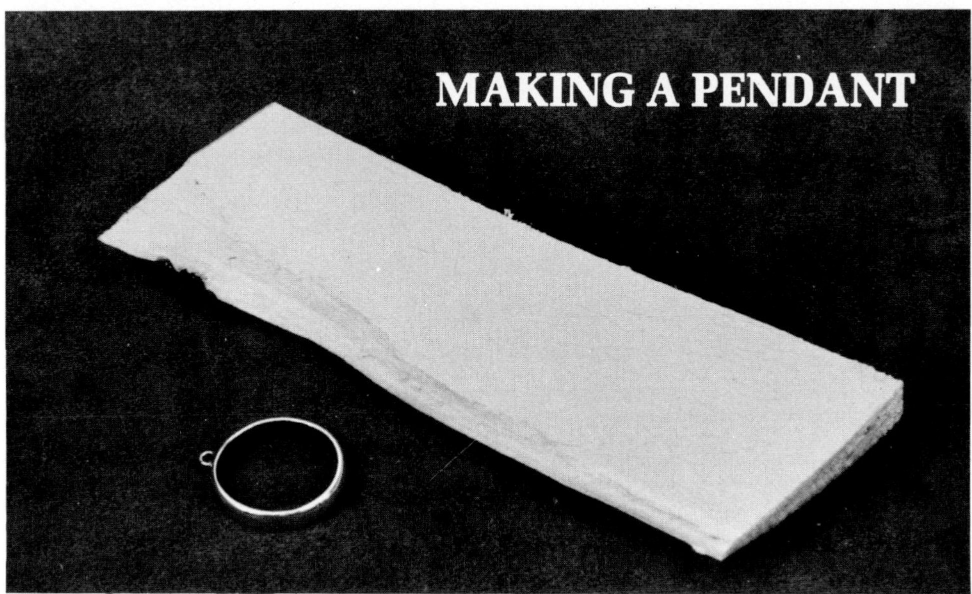

Small scrap pieces of ivory can be put to many uses. One such use is the making of jewelry. For this project we are making a gold pendant with an ivory inlay. The gold ring is actually a wedding band to which we have soldered a small gold ring so that it might be attached to a necklace.

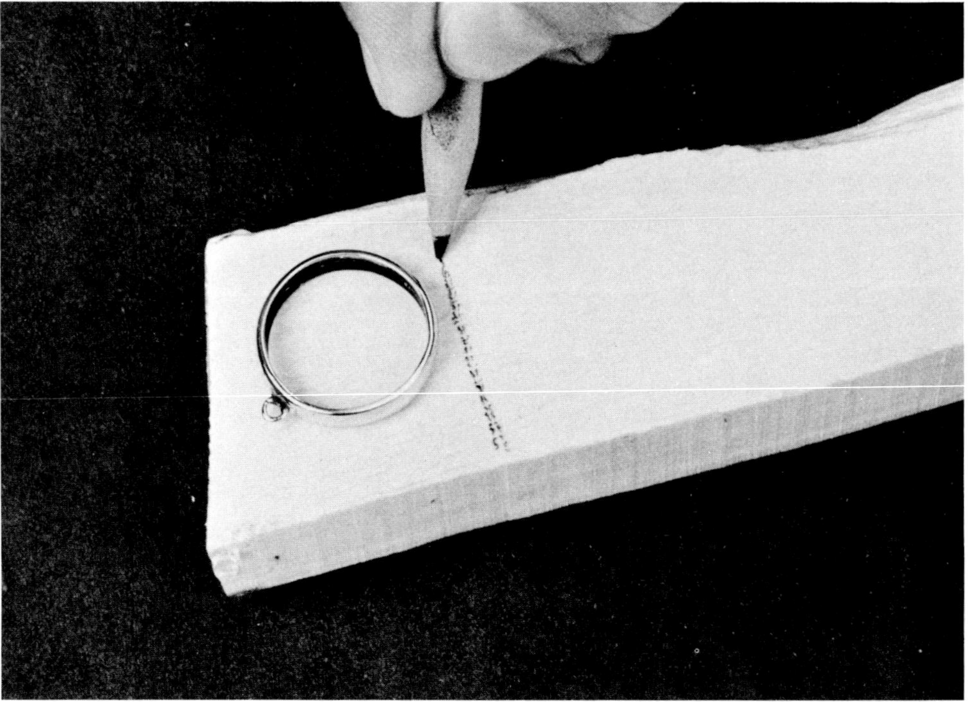

The ring is placed on a piece of ivory so that a portion of suitable size may be marked off. For an inlay of this type, it is necessary that the ivory be somewhat thicker (at least 50%) than the ring.

After the proper sized piece is cut, it must be flattened on each side. The flattened sides must be parallel. We use a belt sander with a coarse grit belt for this purpose. Coarse grit sandpaper will do the same job, but it takes a little longer. If you must use sandpaper, be sure that it is placed on a perfectly flat surface as any irregularities in the surface will transfer to the surface of the ivory.

The ring is placed on the flattened ivory and a sharp pointed lead pencil is used to outline the inlay. A sharp pencil must be used so that the point will mark close to the ring.

The inlay is now cut out and brought to final dimensions with a file. If the outline of the inlay was made correctly, it will be necessary to leave a small white border outside the pencil line. Make certain that the sides of the inlay are cut at a 90 degree angle to the face. A coarse to medium file will give a much better cut than a fine file. Ivory has a tendency to clog a fine file quickly.

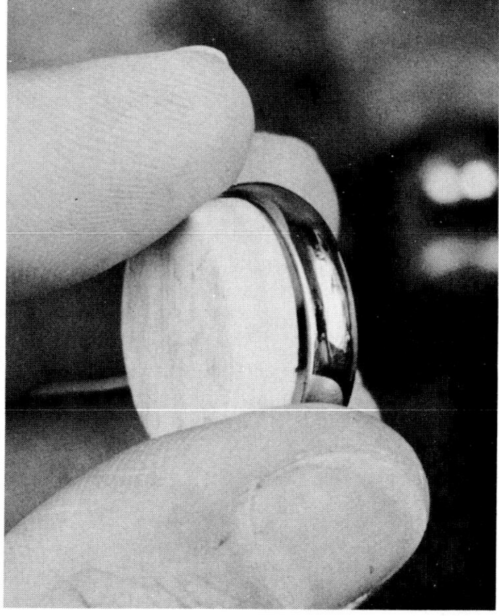

As the inlay is being filed to final shape, it should be frequently placed against the ring to check for size. The proper size should give a tight friction fit. You should not be able to place the inlay in the ring by thumb pressure alone. Use visual inspection to ascertain correct sizing. The inlay is not to be placed into the ring at this stage as it would be very difficult to remove.

Lay the ring and the inlay side by side on a flat surface and mark the ivory at a height equal to half the thickness of the ring. Place the ivory in a vice or similar secure position and with a small triangular file, cut a small groove around the outer circumference. This groove will give the epoxy a good purchase when the inlay is bonded into the ring.

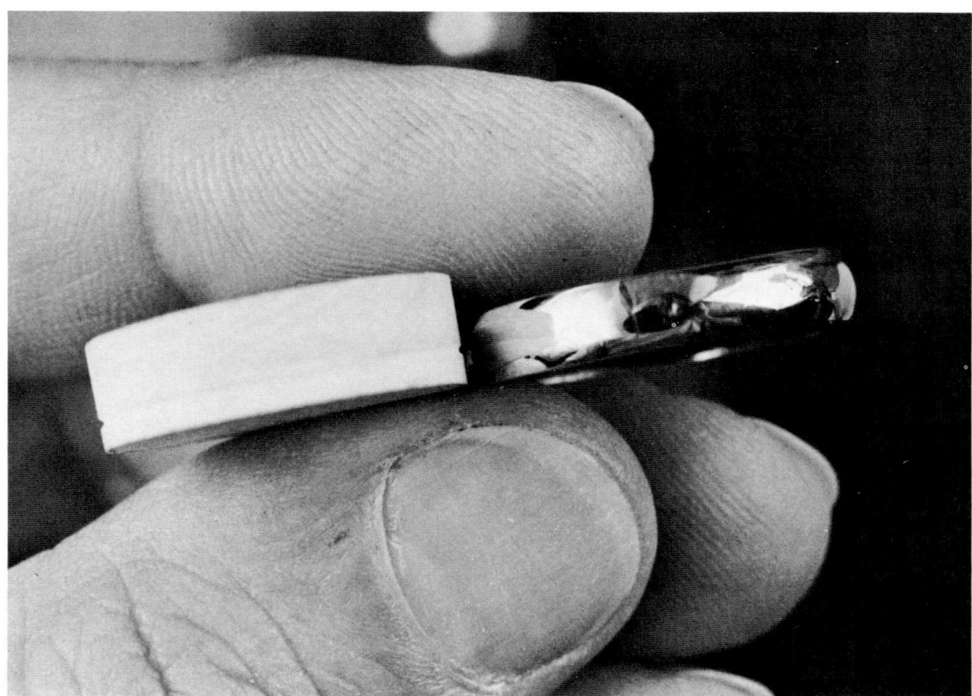

The inside of the ring should be well sanded with a medium grit (150-220) sandpaper. This will slightly score the inside of the ring and will also help make the epoxy bond stronger.

After a liberal amount of epoxy has been applied to the sides of the inlay and the inside of the ring, the inlay should be forced into the ring. This may be done within the jaws of a vice, or with a hammer on a smooth flat surface as illustrated. We use a thin piece of leather under the ring to prevent scratching.

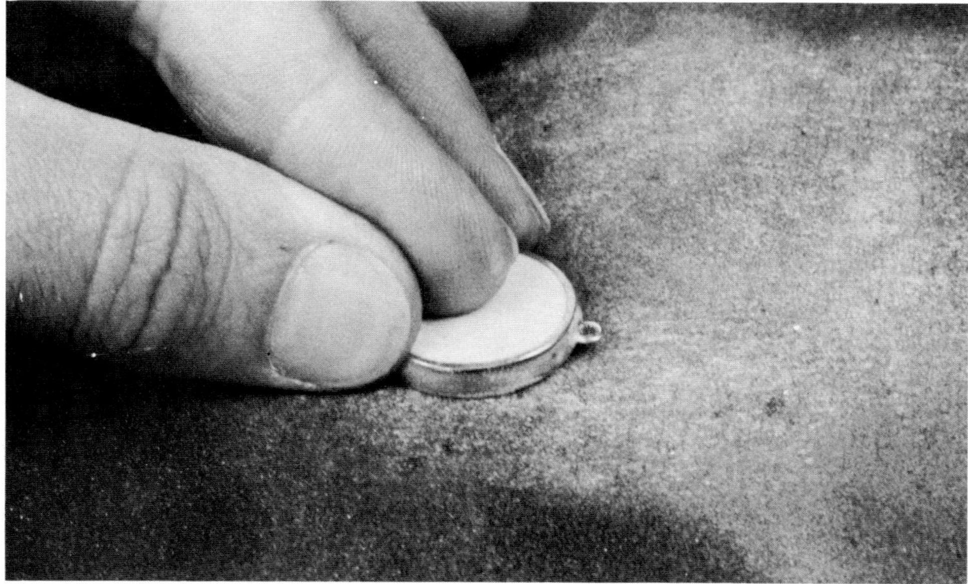

Allow the epoxy to cure. The excess ivory on the top side of the pendant should be sanded off flush with the surface of the ring. Coarse paper should be used until the excess ivory is removed almost to the ring. Fine grit paper should be used to finish up the pendant on both sides prior to buffing. It is absolutely necessary that the sanding be done on a perfectly flat surface.

After sanding to a fine grit finish the ivory inlay is buffed to a mirror finish and is ready for scrimshaw.

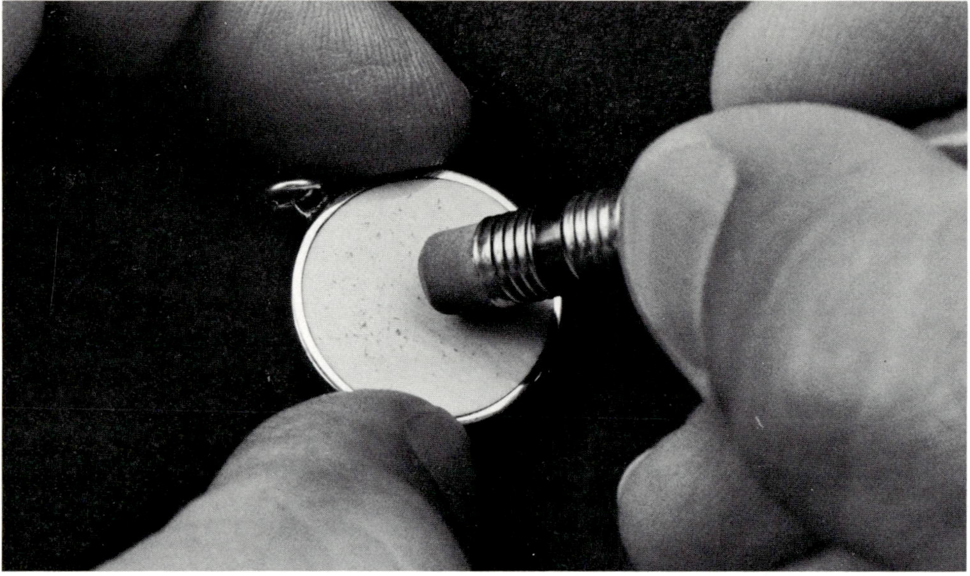

It is almost impossible to draw on the polished ivory with a pencil, so the surface must be prepared. The best way to do this is by rubbing the area thoroughly with a rubber eraser. The erasers which come on the end of most pencils do a good job. The pencil eraser has just the right degree of abrasive quality. It will allow the surface to take the mark of the pencil lead but it will not interfere with the ability of the polished surface to resist the ink.

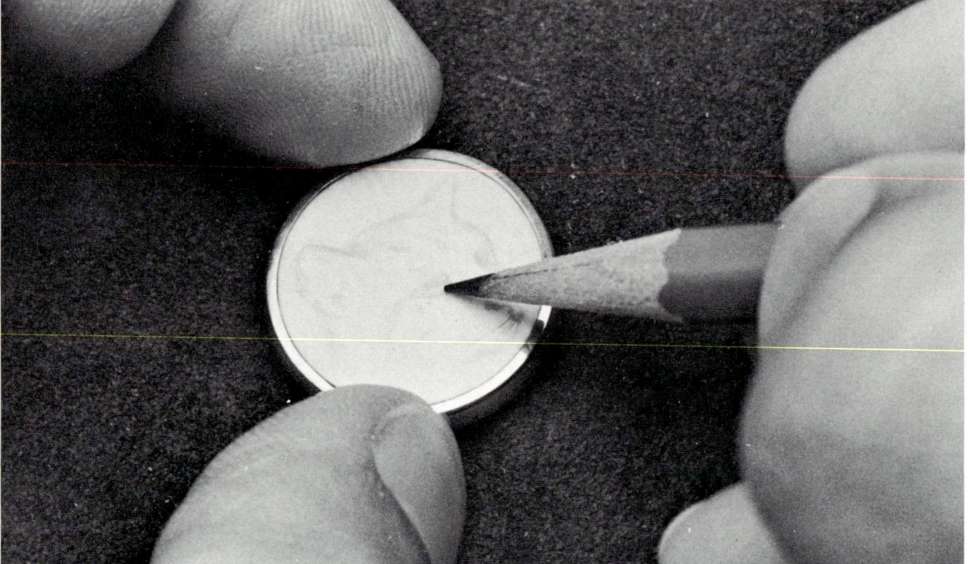

After the surface of the ivory is prepared, the desired scene is laid out with a sharp lead pencil. This drawing need not be exact, however, the exterior dimensions should be as nearly correct as possible. Any detail included at this time is going to be helpful, but anything left out in the preliminary drawing can be added later.

The pencil drawing is highly susceptible to smearing and it must be protected during the scrimshaw process. An acrylic spray coating such as Krylon should be applied over the drawing. This coating of acrylic should be thin, but it must be evenly applied so that the complete scene is protected. The scrimshaw tool will cut through this protective coating and the coloring agent can be applied and wiped away without disturbing the rest of the artwork. Make sure that the acrylic coating is thoroughly dry before the actual carving is begun.

Now it's time to use the scrimshaw tool. The first cut should be a very light line which outlines the drawing.

After the drawing is outlined, ink is applied to the ivory. We use Higgins waterproof india ink. It is only necessary to use about one drop and the applicator in the bottle makes a good dispenser.

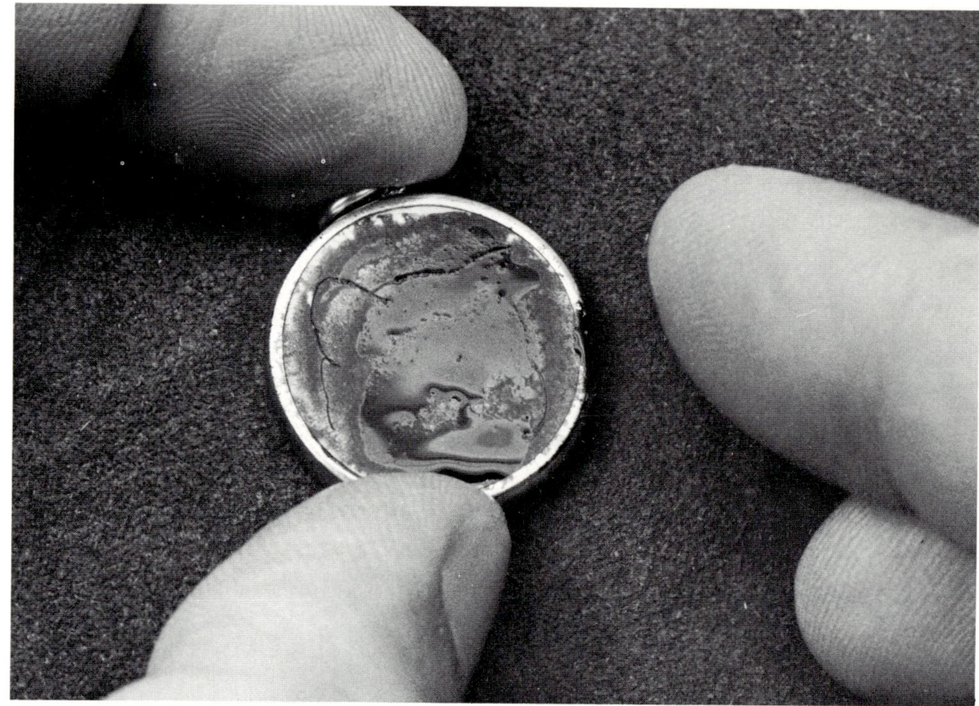

The ink should be rubbed thoroughly into the cut and it can be wiped off of the ivory immediately. A folded piece of paper towel moistened with saliva does a good job and is convenient to use. When the excess ink has been removed, the cut should stand out nice and clear.

Now begins the process of cut, ink, rub, and wipe. The acrylic spray has protected the pencil drawing and we are still able to use this drawing as a guide for our basic cuts, however, we will immediately begin to add extra detail. The initial outline cuts do not represent the actual physical appearance of cat fur, so the solid line must be replaced with a more realistic representation. In this greatly enlarged photograph, we can see the small white cuts which are made through the outline of the left ear. These small cuts will give the visual effect of fur and will be made around the entire outline. The cuts on the cat's head between the ears are made to follow the contour of the head. From this point, all cuts should be made to follow the natural contours of the subject. Depressed or raised areas may be represented by cuts which cross each other (cross hatch).

As the detail begins to grow and the number of cuts begin to add up, it can become difficult to see each new cut as it is made. By adding ink to the uncut areas the white mark of each new cut is highly visible. This excess ink can be added to the whole surface of the ivory or it may be applied to specific areas with a small brush or a cotton swab.

The young lady who is wearing the pendant pointed out the fact that our cat had no whiskers. The finished cat below (shown actual size) is complete with whiskers.

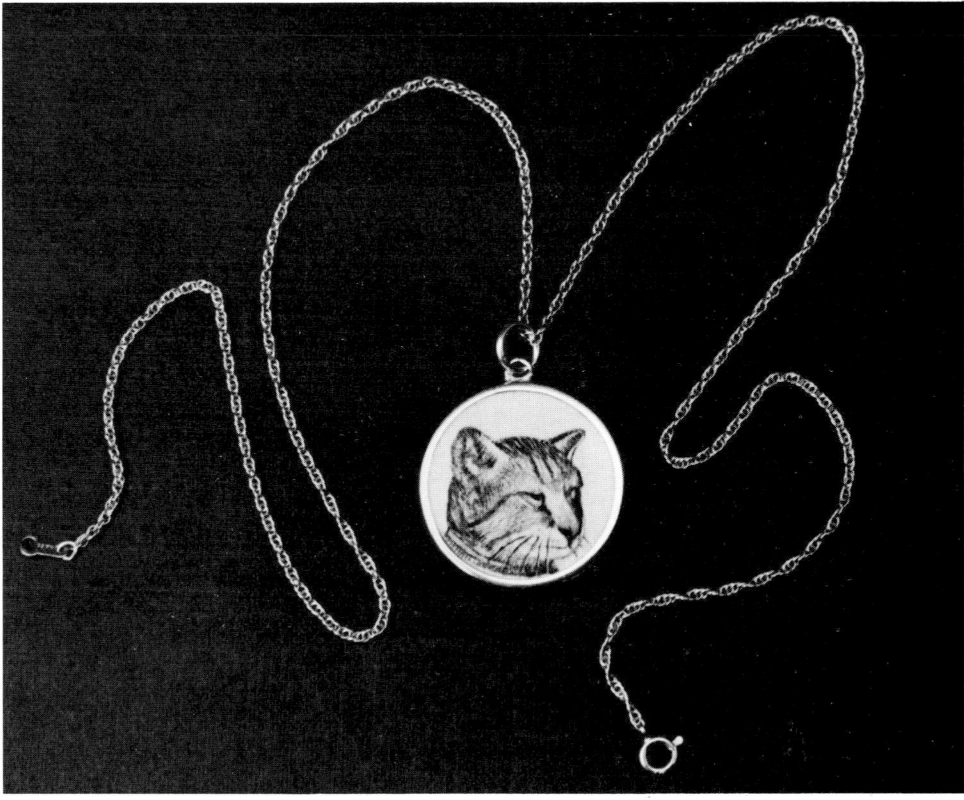

HANDGUN GRIPS

Ivory has always been a popular material for the grips of fine pistols. Revolvers and automatics alike can be made more attractive with a nice set of ivory grips and ivory has proven to be a durable as well as beautiful material for this purpose. Bo Trahan, of Kenner, Louisiana, chose ivory grips to compliment the tasteful scroll engraving on his Smith & Wesson Model 60 revolver. The Model 60 is a stainless steel handgun with a bright satin finish. An arrangement of yellow roses was decided upon as a fitting subject for the artist.

The grips were furnished ready made by Mr. Trahan and they were inspected to determine if further work would be necessary to prepare them for scrimshaw. The finish as received was excellent and the first actual task of the artist (after removal from the revolver) was to prepare the surface for the preliminary pencil sketch. The surface of each grip was rubbed thoroughly with a rubber eraser and the sketch was made.

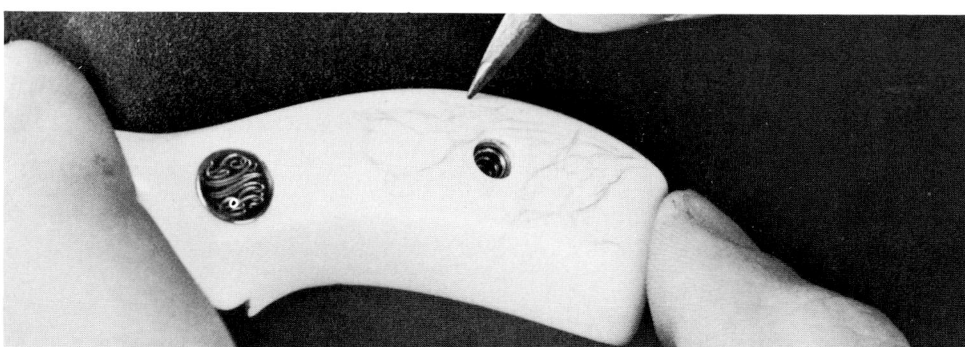

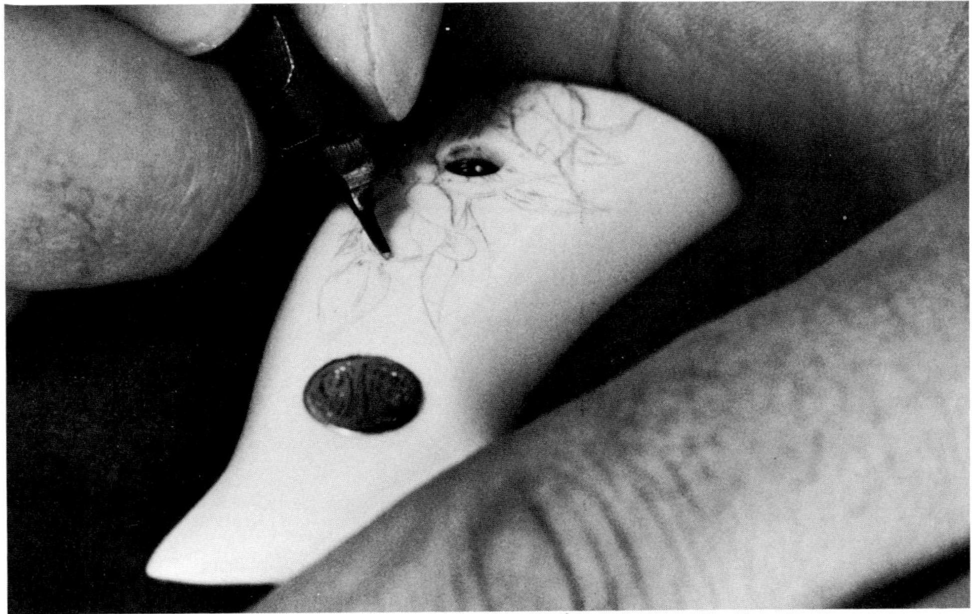

After the grip is sprayed with a coating of Krylon, it is allowed to dry and the outline of the sketch is cut in.

Black india ink is rubbed into the cuts and cleaned off with a moistened paper towel. The resulting outline appears rough and uneven but the unevenness is caused by the tendency of the acrylic coating to chip away in places as the ivory is cut. This is of no concern, because the purpose of the coating is only to prevent the pencil marks from being wiped away prematurely. The india ink will occasionally seep into little crevices caused by the chipping of the acrylic but it is removed when the acrylic coating is removed.

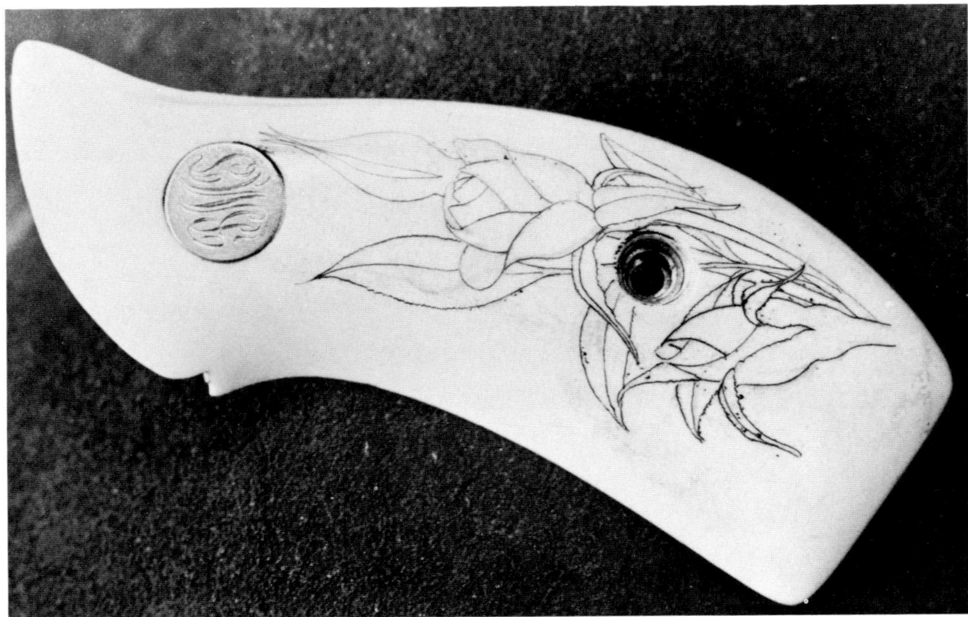

Prior to coloring, the acrylic coating must be removed. Removal of the coating with nail polish remover has little or no effect on the black ink but the colored ink is much more susceptible to damage. The acrylic should be completely removed and the surface of the ivory should be washed thoroughly with a mild soap or detergent and dried immediately.

Since this carving is to be in full color, it is now necessary to prepare certain areas of the carving to accept the colored ink. The areas which are to be finished in a solid color are prepared by cutting a series of overlapping lines which fill the total space to be colored. These slightly overlapping lines should be cut to the contours of the subject. The cuts in a leaf should start at the center and flow outward to the edge on each side. The cuts in the stems should run the length of the stem, and the cuts in the roses should follow the gentle curves of each petal.

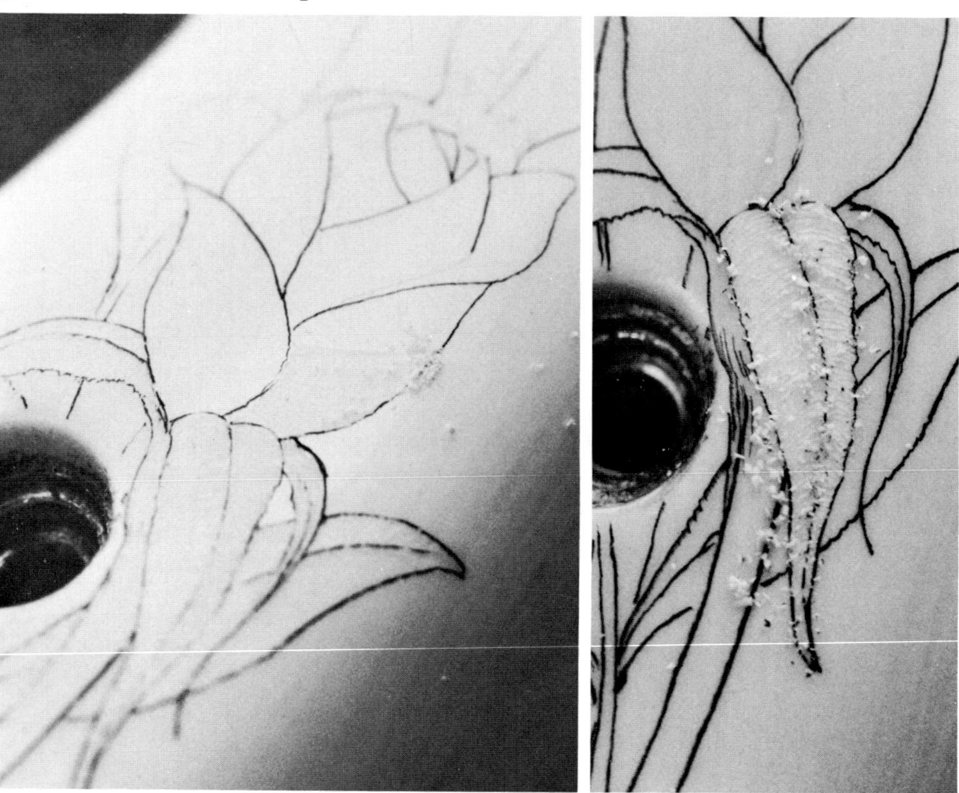

As the areas to be colored are cut in, there is an obvious amount of ivory removed from the surface. These ivory shavings are evidence of the superiority of the use of a cutting tool as opposed to the use of a pointed tool. The enlarged photographs show the symmetry of the overlapping lines which is possible with a cutting tool. A pointed tool would give an entanglement of scratches which would be great for carving a likeness of a bird's nest but less than satisfactory for roses.

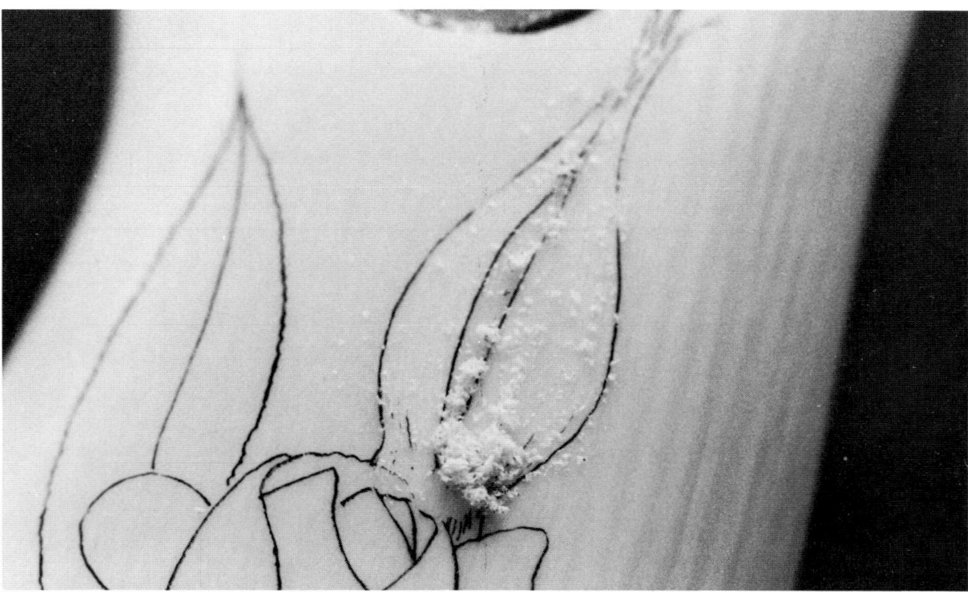

The cut areas can now be inked in for color. A 0000 sable brush is best for this job. If a brush of this size is impossible to locate, a suitable size can be obtained by carefully removing some of the outside bristles on a 000 sable brush. The small brush is necessary for the detail work needed for realism.

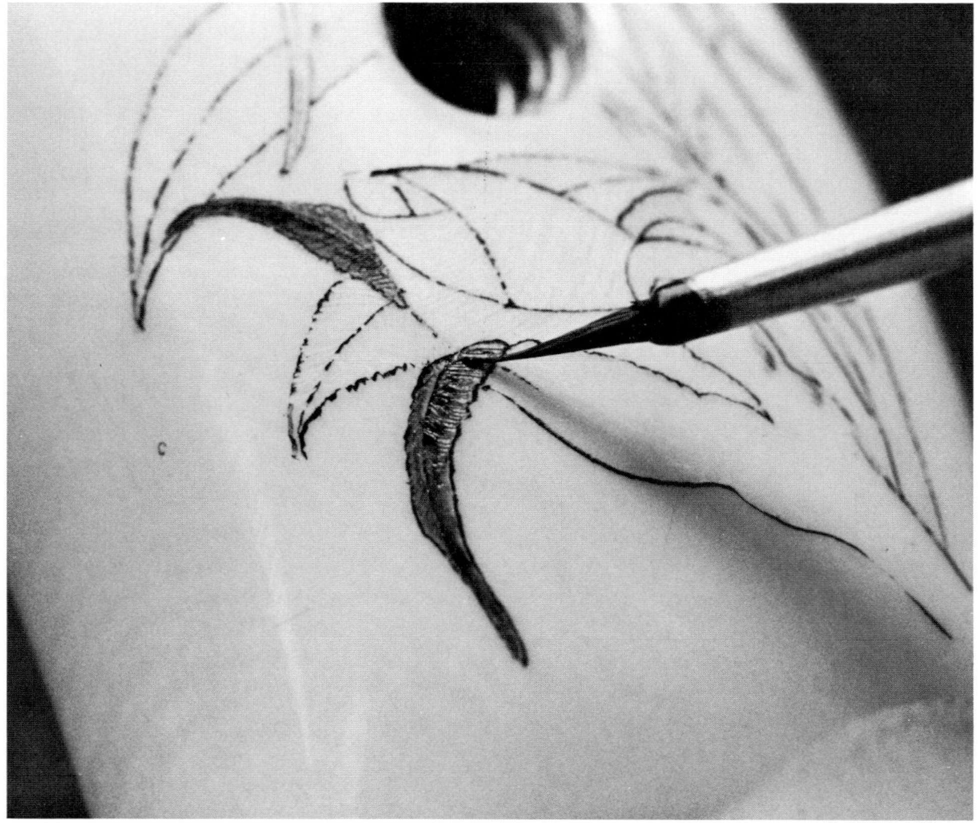

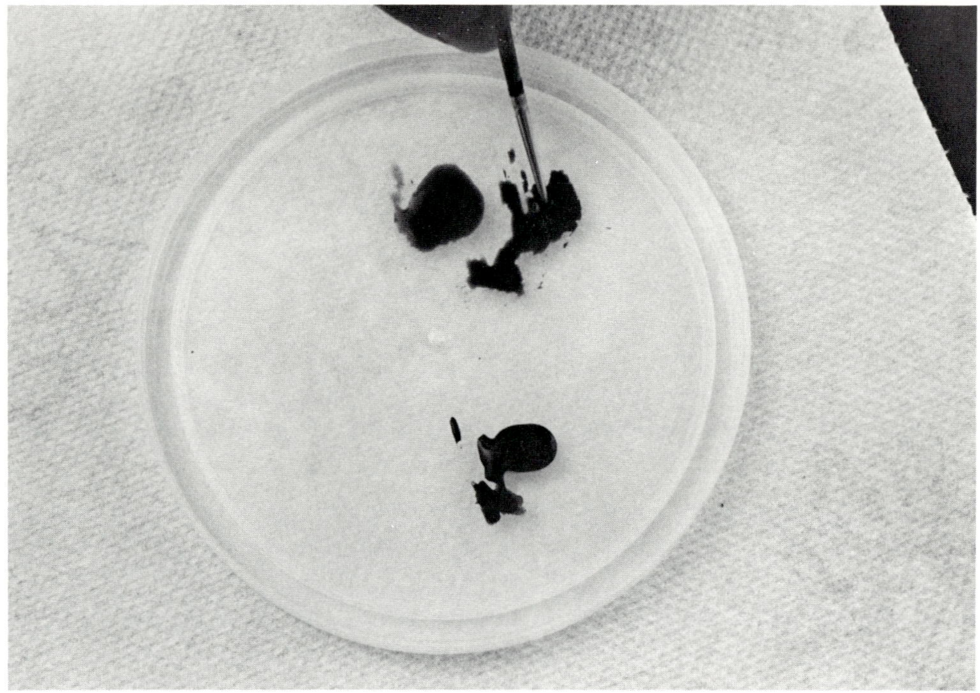

All of the colors in the rainbow are available from a few bottles of Higgins ink. Basic colors are placed on a smooth white surface such as a dish or saucer. In this illustration, we are using a transparent plastic top which is placed over a piece of white paper. It is necessary to have the white background in order to see the true quality of the mixed colors. The colors are mixed with the tip of the brush until correct and then applied to the ivory.

Colored areas can be highlighted by light cuts with the scrimshaw tool. The resulting fine white lines can blend into the color giving a natural and realistic effect.

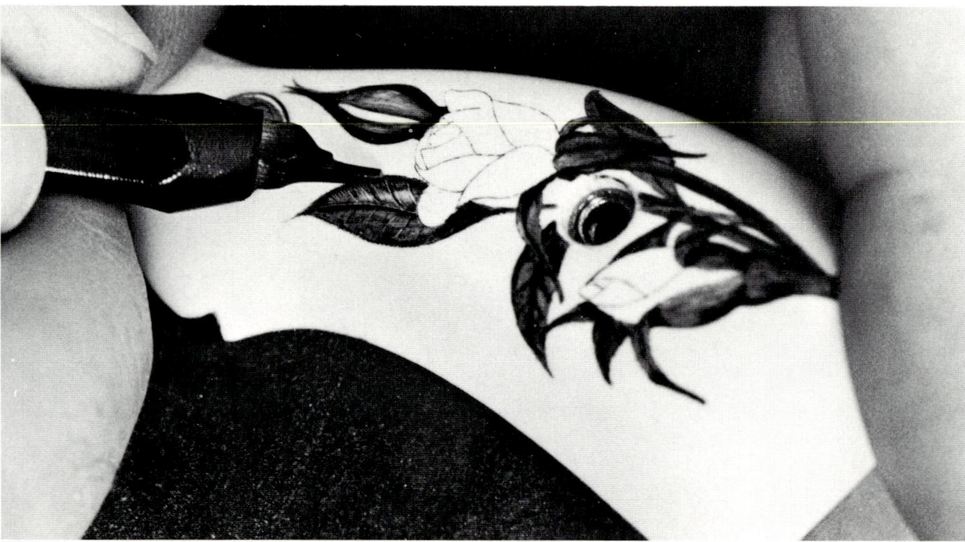

Each different color must be carefully applied to its designated area only. Any overlapping or blending of the colors could ruin the carving. Remember that darker colors will always overpower lighter colors. A little yellow run over into the black area wouldn't present a problem, but a little black over into the yellow would mean that the area would have to be cleaned up with the scrimshaw tool and started over.

The last step is to sign the work. The artist's name is cut into the ivory and black ink is rubbed in. Since the black ink is going to be placed next to the light green leaves and rose buds, extreme caution must be used to see that the black ink does not touch the colored area. When removing the black ink it must be wiped away from the colored area carefully.

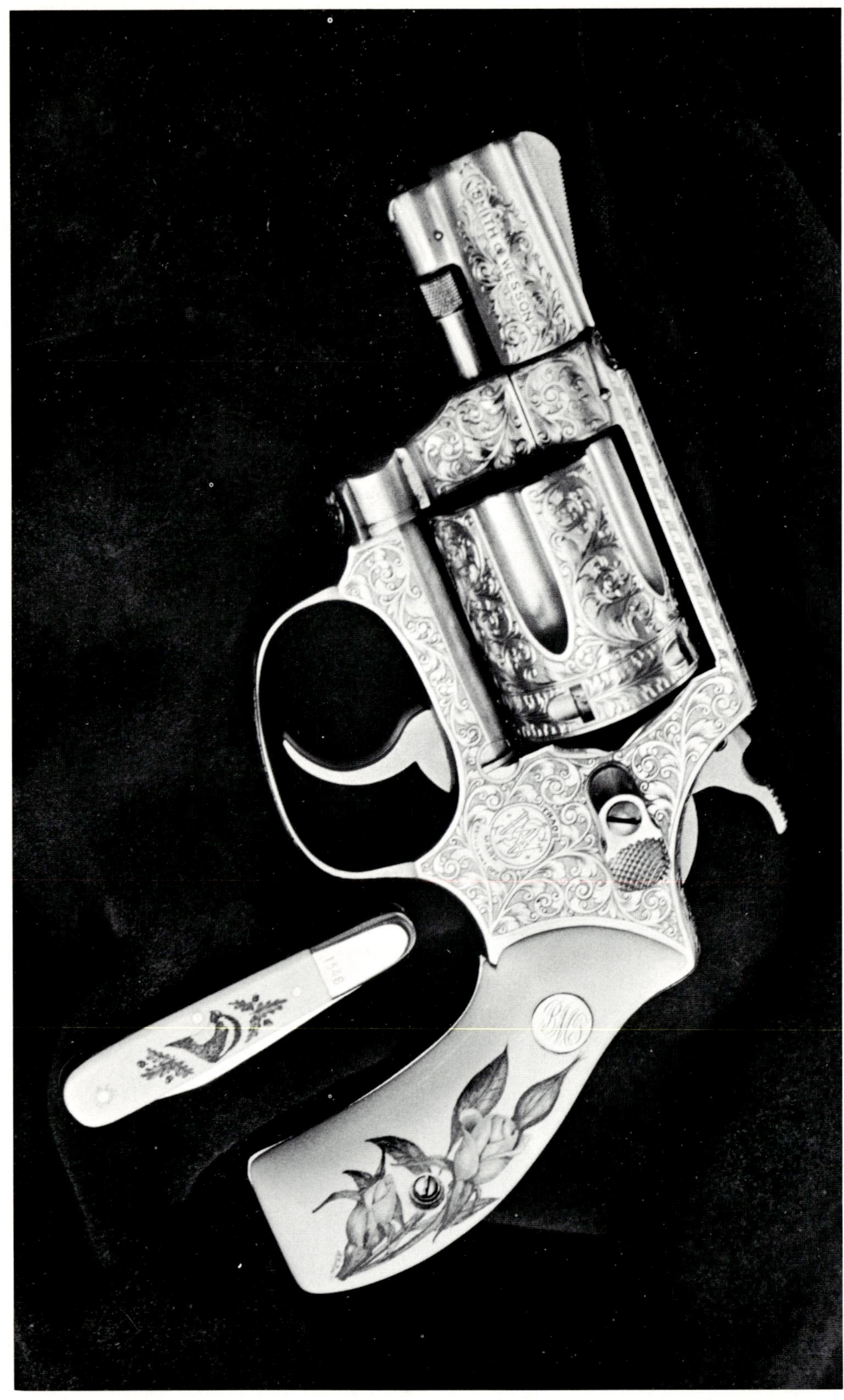

This eagle carved into the grip of a Colt 45 automatic pistol shows excellent detail. The feathers were prepared for coloring with literally thousands of cuts. Each small feather might have 30 to 50 individual cuts and they are all overlapped properly to give a fully colored surface.

WOOD DUCK ON A BELT BUCKLE

It is very helpful to hold the ivory so that the light will aid in the carving. A plain white cut against a white background is very difficult to see but the shadow caused by angled lighting makes the same cut stand out clearly.

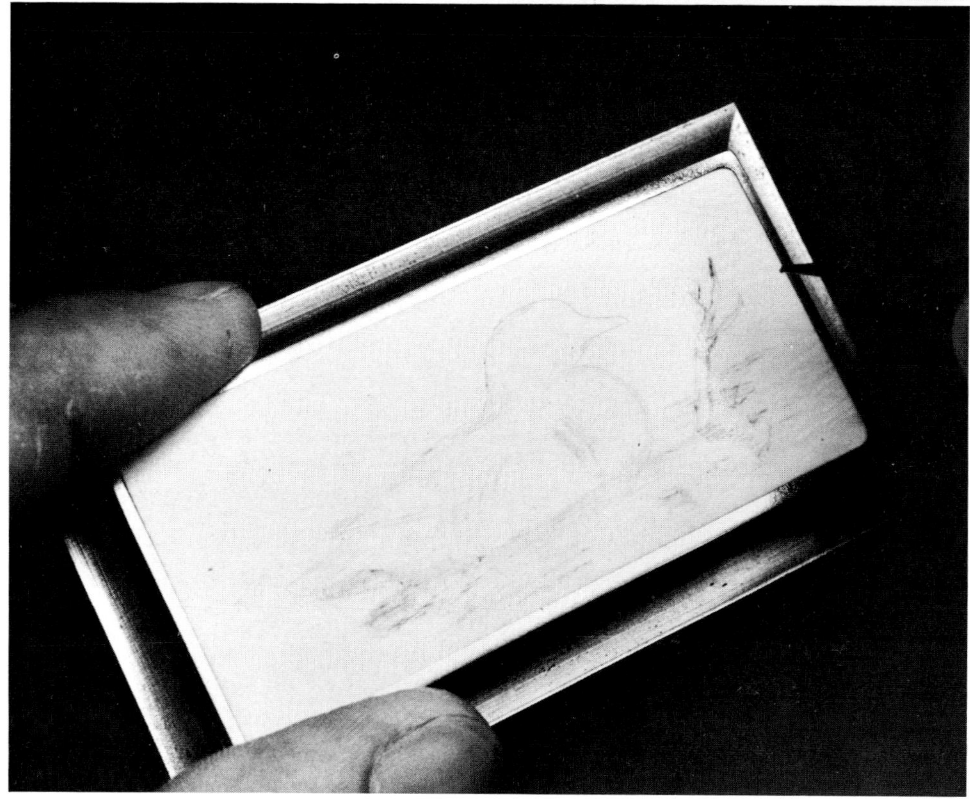

The shadow of the duck and the branch sticking up out of the water helps add realism to what could be an uninteresting scene.

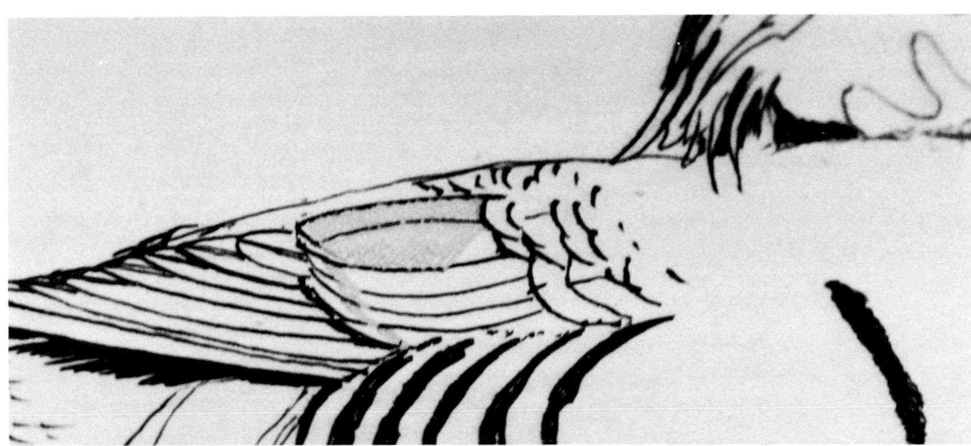

Working one area at a time is usually a good idea. Cutting in and coloring the feathers individually makes the work less boring and also helps with detail.

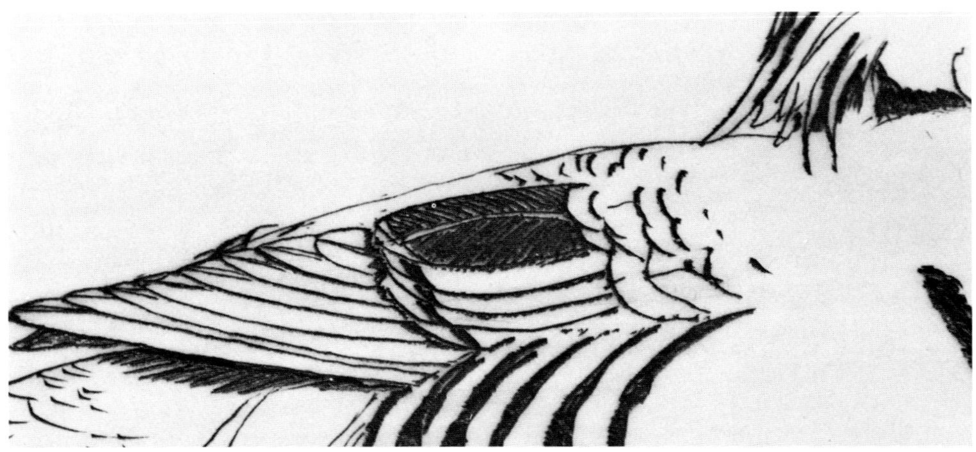

Cutting in the head for coloring.

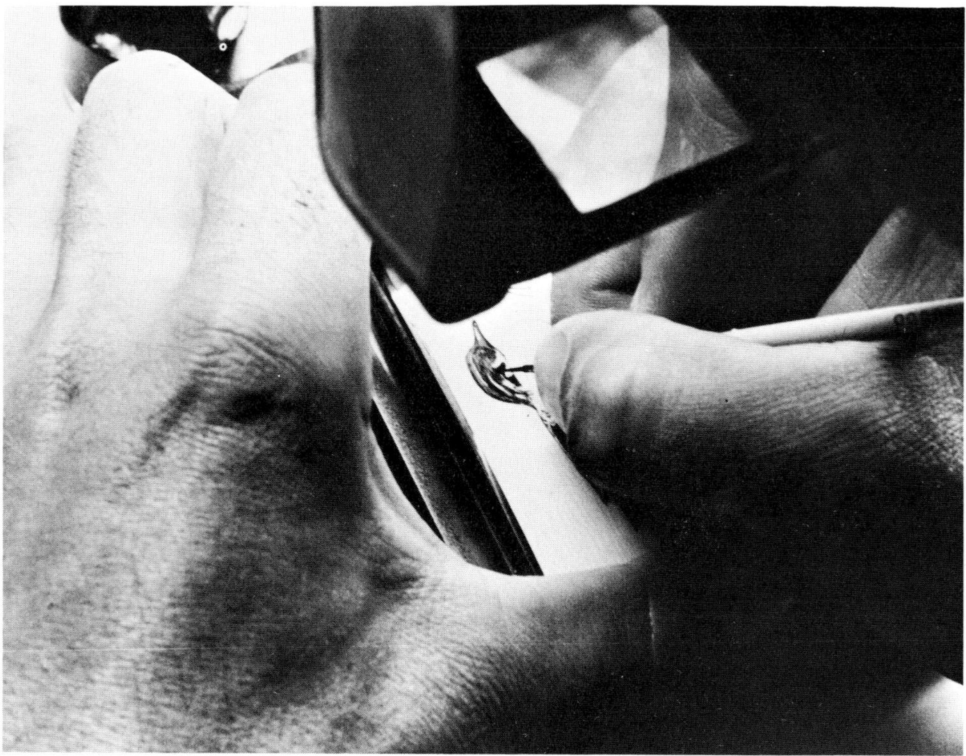

Using the 00000 sable brush to apply color to the head.

Cutting in the breast for coloring.

After the breast has been colored, small feathers can be given individual detail by cutting light white cuts out against the darker background.

The artist's name is added last and again we emphasize the necessity of keeping the black ink out of the colored areas.

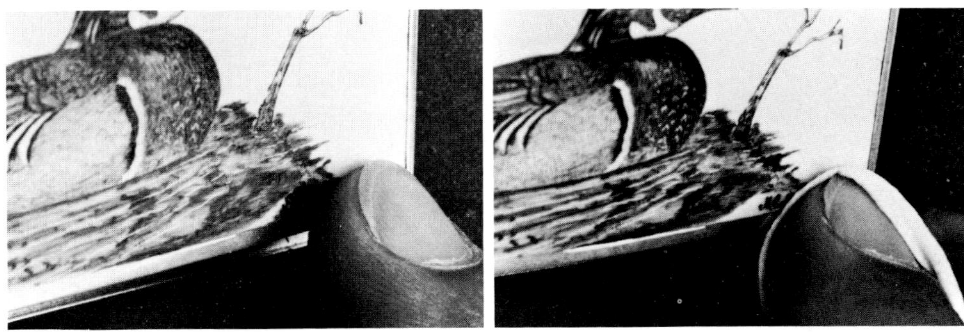

The finished buckle is beautiful and useful too. It is actually the handle of a high quality folding knife which serves the dual purposes of belt buckle and emergency tool or weapon.

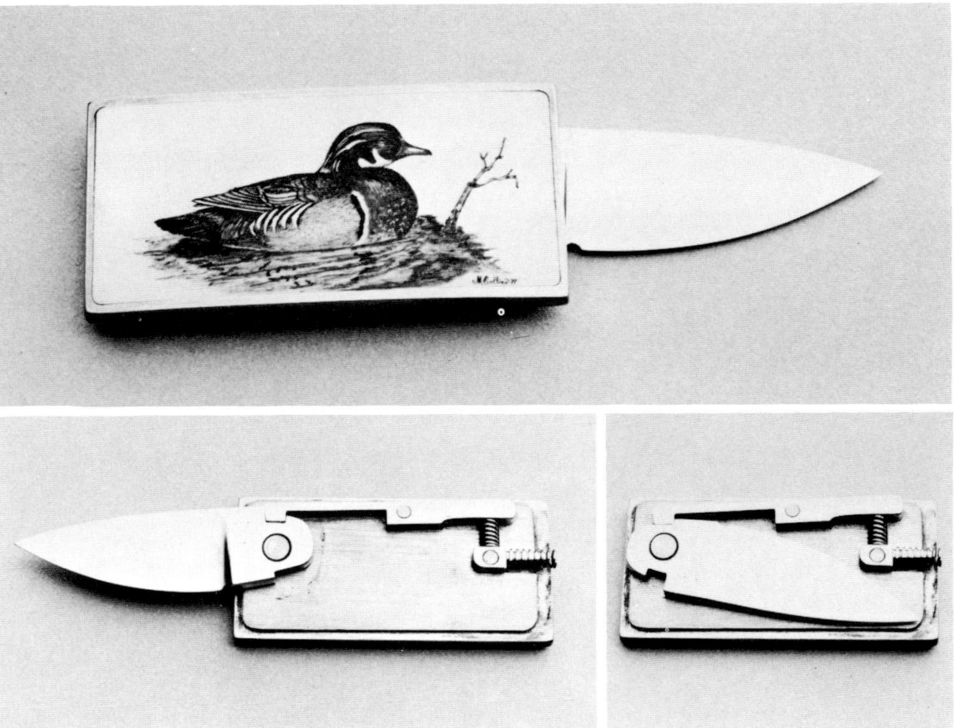

The most typical scrimshaw is a sailing vessel on a sperm whale tooth. The sperm whale tooth is very rough except for the tip of the tooth which protrudes from the jawbone. This smooth tip accounts for only ¼ or less of the total length of the tooth and the rough remainder must be prepared before carving. After the proper area is smoothed and polished, the art can be laid out for scrimshaw.

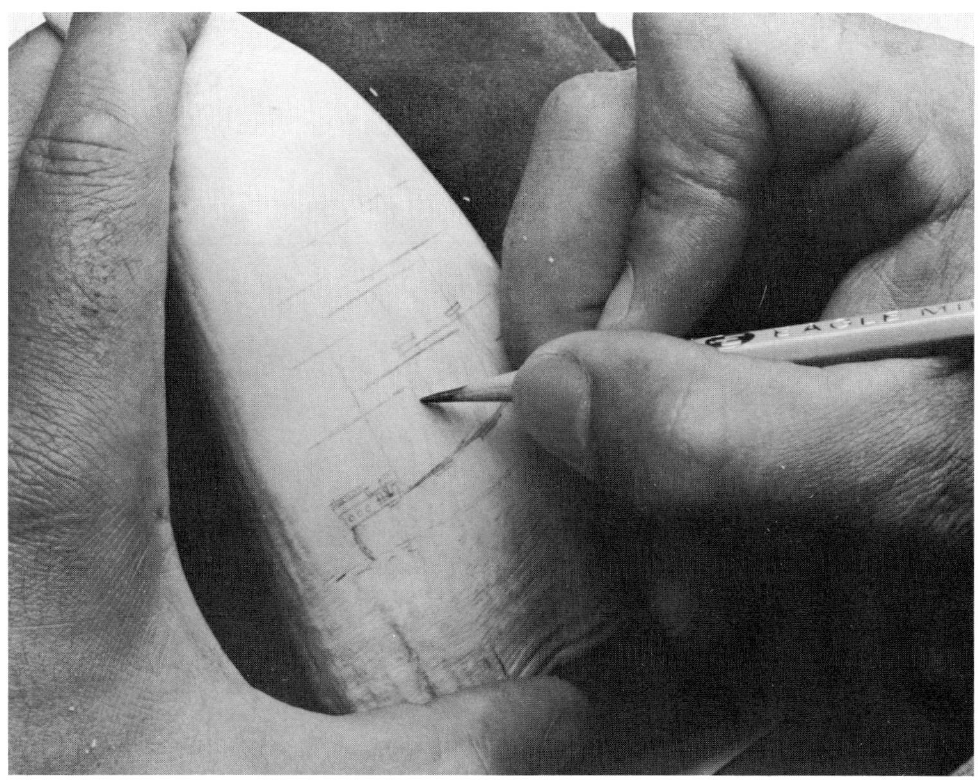

Spraying the pencil artwork with Krylon.

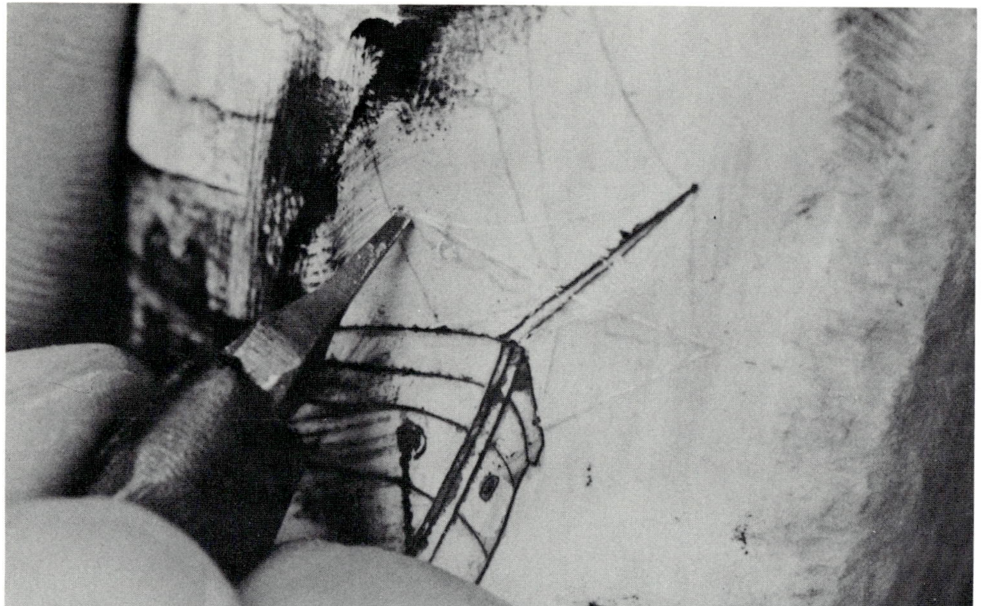

Cutting in the lines.

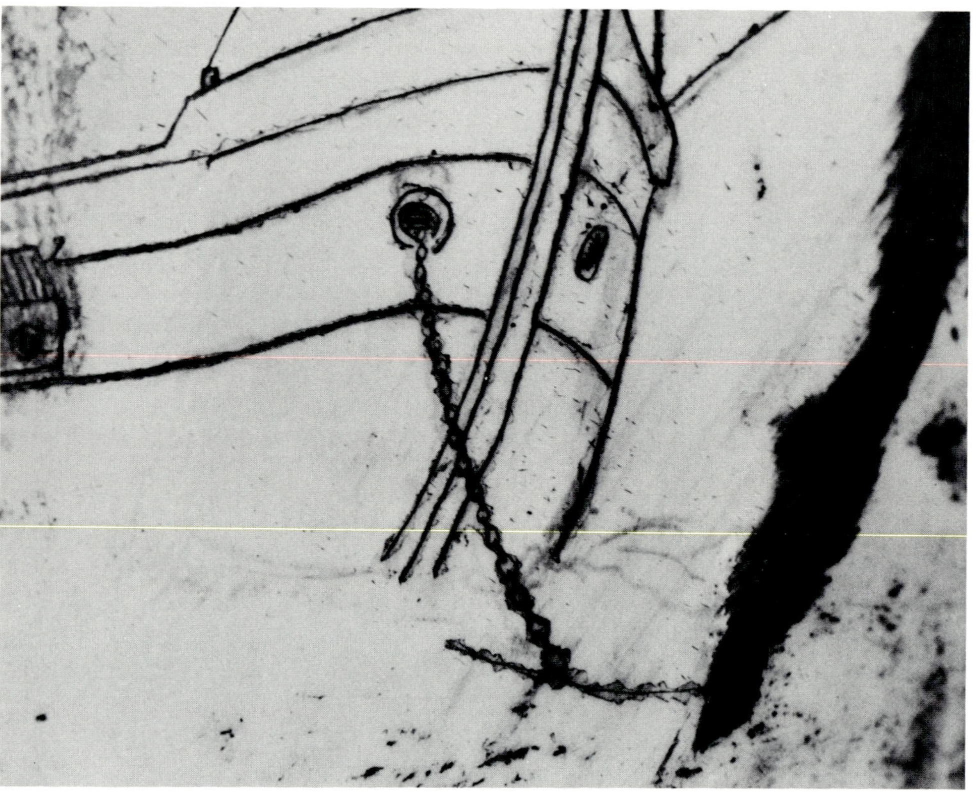

Closeup showing detail of anchor chain. This photograph illustrates the rough appearance caused by the ink flowing into the edges of the acrylic coating where it has torn away from the scrimshaw tool during the cutting.

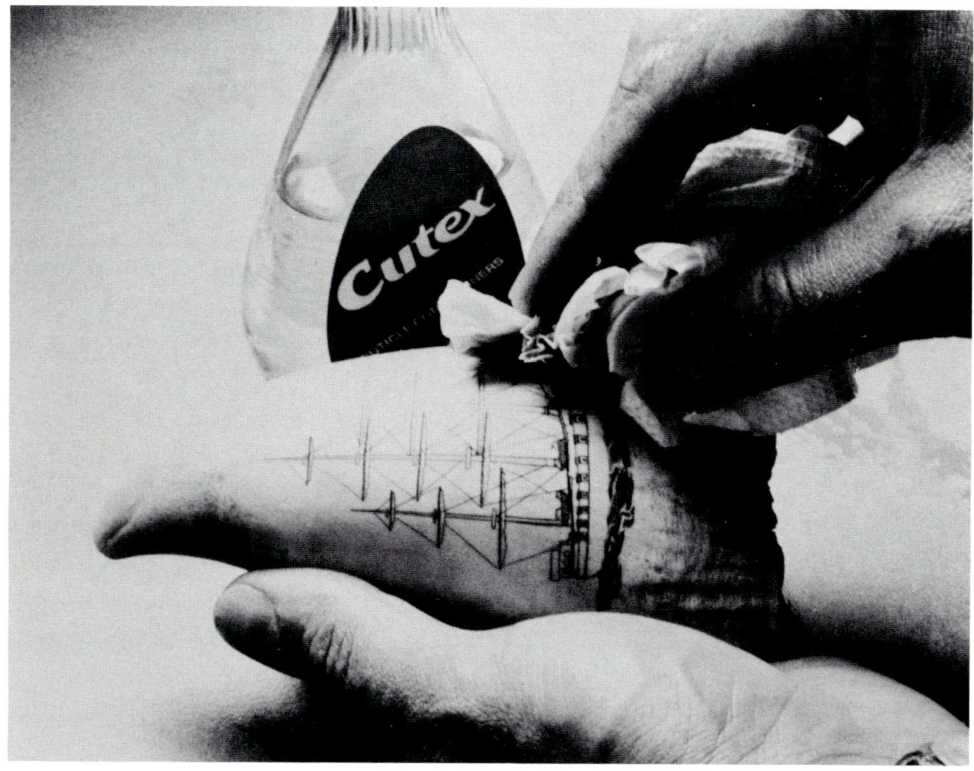

Cleaning away the acrylic coating after the basic cuts have been made. First, nail polish remover, and then, soapy water.

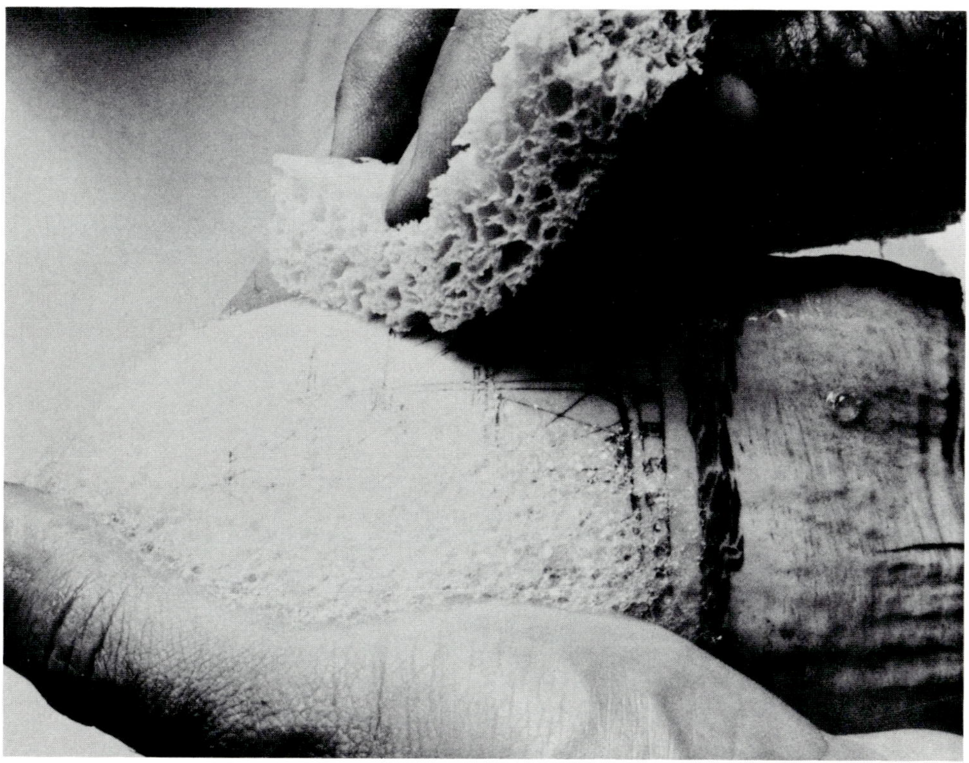

Ink is lightly smeared over the scene to provide a better view of the small cuts in the rigging.

The details of the wooden structure of the hull are cut in.

Enlarged photograph shows details of waves and water splashing against the hull.

The finished tooth is very much like those which were carved by the early whaling seamen.

TIPS ON SCRIMSHAW

Use a soft and flexible surface to hold the object which is being worked. A bean bag made up of soft suede leather and filled with gravel is excellent. This bag will allow you to change the position and angle of the ivory to suit the different cuts and lighting requirements.

Use adequate lighting and take advantage of shadows to see exactly where each cut is placed.

The first cut should always be a light outline of the whole scene and the major components of the scene.

Always draw the desired artwork out on the ivory prior to cutting. It can save a lot of time and ivory.

Learn to hold and use the scrimshaw tool as you would a pen or pencil. It should feel natural in your hand and its use should require very little pressure. If it takes more than a little pressure to make the proper cuts, the tool is dull or you are doing something wrong. Most cuts need no more pressure than a ball point pen does for writing.

Always use a sharp tool. If you have any reason to believe that the tool is dull...stop...sharpen it now. Don't wait!

Never get ivory too hot to hold comfortably in your bare hands.

Do not store ivory in a hot, dry place. It will dry out and crack.

Never soak ivory in water or leave it wet for any length of time. When you wash it - dry it immediately.

Never start to carve a piece of ivory unless you are absolutely sure that the surface has been properly prepared. Properly prepared means perfectly smooth with no scratches or rough areas.

Handle colored work very carefully until it has had adequate time to dry. Black ink doesn't give any problems but some of the lighter colors are delicate and must be handled accordingly.

While working on a large scene, don't skip around. Work one area at a time and finish it before you start on another.

Michael Collins is a nationally recognized wildlife artist who also specializes in the art of scrimshaw. For several years, he has been one of the country's foremost custom knife makers and most of his knives have ivory handles upon which he executes his beautiful scrimshaw work. Michael's scrimshaw is sought after by art enthusiasts and collectors who consider his work unique and of superb quality.

Walter "Blackie" Collins is a weapons designer and the author of several books related to his field. He and his brother, Michael, became interested in scrimshaw several years ago as a means of decorating their custom knives. While Blackie does very little scrimshaw himself, the gold and ivory pendant illustrated in this book was done by him for Margaret Booth, the daughter of a close friend.